Rile and Gridley

# Rile and Gridley

∽

## Written and Illustrated by
## Ryan Thiele

Copyright © 2021 by Ryan Thiele

All rights reserved. No part of this book may be reproduced in any manner whatsoever without written permission except in the case of brief quotations embodied in critical articles and reviews.

First Printing, 2021

"The hot chocolate or cupcakes?" asked Roxy.
"What will surprise the boys most?"
"I'm not sure, " answered Veronica Fox.
"But I just stepped in something gross."

From behind the red door
A loud commotion filled the hall,
Rattling the dust and the cobwebs
And the posters on the wall.

Roxy Raccoon was puzzled.
"What *are* the boys *UP* to?"
"Definitely not cleaning,"
Veronica knew.

"Gridley! Stop!" the girls shouted.
"Don't hurt your best friend!"

The boys turned and laughed.
"Hey Girls! Come on in!"

Gridley explained,
"We were rehearsing a scene.
Auditions are tomorrow.
I was *pretending* to be mean."

"We are really sorry," Rile said.
"That we made your hearts stir.
"But this means our acting must rock!"
Then Gridley slapped Rile some fur.

"Though once," said Gridley,
"A long time ago
I did, in fact,
Knock Rile to the floor."

"We weren't always best friends,"
Rile had to admit.
And without saying more
Into a cupcake he bit.

But the girls were confused
For this story they'd not heard.
Rile and Gridley not friends?
The idea was absurd!

Rile then explained,
While Gridley nibbled and ate,
That their strong friendship began
Due to happenstance and fate.

"Our hero, Twyman Buckley,
From old movies and TV shows,
Actually brought out similarities
We had and didn't even know!"

Rile continued and said,
"Gridley was popular in school.
But to those who were different
He was awfully cruel."

"Being cool," Gridley admitted,
"Meant a complete disregard
For the feelings of others.
Tolerating me must have been hard."

"So one can imagine," said Rile,
"How funny it was
To see Mr. Big Shot covered
In dirt, grime, and fuzz!"

"It wasn't *that* funny.
But Rile wouldn't stop.
His laughter was obnoxious
And I really blew my top.

"So, nose first,
Right into a locker
I forcefully sent
That irritating mocker!

"But when I left Rile
In a lump on the floor,
I discovered something
I didn't know before.

"'Twyman Buckley fan, huh?'
I asked, ignoring a hateful look."
"He's my favorite actor," snarled Rile.
"Now get your trash-hands off my book."

"Sometime," said Gridley,
"I'd like to borrow this from you.
Twyman Buckley, you see,
Is my favorite actor, too."

"But I didn't believe him,"
Rile explained more.
"I thought he was teasing
And I planned to even the score.

"So imagine how shocking,
After a few days went by,
When Gridley arrived
Just to say, 'hi!'"

"Have you seen this movie?" asked Gridley.
Rile confessed he had not.
"Found it at a yard sale!
An awesome deal I got!"

"They say it's a classic," said Rile.
"But is it any good?"
Gridley shook his head.
"I'd watch if I could."

The boys started talking and
Gridley's cool facade disappeared.
His parents didn't allow movies.
"A waste of time!" they sneered.

Rile felt sorry for Gridley.
Then... an idea suddenly beamed.
"We'll have a movie night at MY house!
With Twyman Buckley on the screen!"

But Rile didn't know
If the invitation Gridley would take.
Would he actually come over?
A new friend would he make?

But the next Friday night,
After the big football game,
Gridley indeed took a chance
And to Rile's party he came.

"With snacks and a movie
And laughter galore...

"I was the happiest," Gridley said,
"I'd ever been before."

After that night
Rile and Gridley soon became
Inseparable pals--
One and the same.

To become great actors,
They soon discovered,
Was what they both wanted.
And, before long, their talents were uncovered.

They studied day and night
With accents and lines.
They learned how to perform.
They even learned how to mime!

They practiced as characters
Of all shapes and sizes,
Fooling family and friends
With make-up and disguises.

Then, after high school,
To Loud Bark City they moved.
Drilled by the great Osborne Goatlick,
Their acting skills were improved.

"And that's our story,"
Rile continued to say.
"Two ambitious actors--
Without very much pay."

After their tale
Gridley said with regret,
"Sorry, Rile. I was a jerk.
I owe you a debt."

"Thanks for the apology,
But it's not necessary now.
I eventually got you back.
It's in the past, anyhow."

"Got me back?" said Gridley.
"What did you do?"
Then Rile sheepishly grinned
Because Gridley hadn't a clue.

"After being kicked into that locker
You I truly DID NOT LIKE.
So...I took out my feelings
On your new, fancy bike."

"The gum!!! That was *you*???!!!
I couldn't even pedal! I couldn't even steer!
I scraped gum for a *month*!"
"Darn," laughed Rile. "I had hoped for a year!"

Gridley let out a growl.
"Your bones I'm going to crunch!"
Then Veronica told Roxy,
"That's our cue to go to lunch."

"Do you think we should worry," asked Roxy,
"About their hitting and smacking?"

"Nah," said Veronica. "Knowing Rile and Gridley,
They're probably just acting."

**About the author/illustrator:** Ryan Thiele currently lives near Washington, D.C. with his wife, daughter, and dog (a West Highland White Terrier whose look inspired the design of Gridley Fox). Ryan and his wife, Bethany, teach art at the same middle school where their art classrooms are next door to each other. Ryan graduated from the University of Illinois with a degree in painting and further studied art and animation in Los Angeles. He grew up in a small town in Illinois where he spent most of his time drawing, watching movies, and playing with action figures. His childhood home still stands on the corner of Rile and Gridley streets.

CPSIA information can be obtained
at www.ICGtesting.com
Printed in the USA
LVHW072025140821
695342LV00006B/144